# Sew
# Useful

First published in Great Britain 2015

Search Press Limited
Wellwood, North Farm Road,
Tunbridge Wells, Kent TN2 3DR

Photographs by Garie Hind

ISBN: 978-1-78221-085-6

**Suppliers**
For details of suppliers, please visit
the Search Press website:
www.searchpress com.

Printed in China

# Sew
# Useful

### 23 simple storage solutions to sew for the home

**Debbie Shore**

SEARCH PRESS

# Contents

*Small Case,
page 28*

*Garment Cover,
page 32*

*Iron Caddy,
page 36*

*Knitting Needle Roll,
page 56*

*Pen Case,
page 58*

*Hoop Basket,
page 60*

*Gift Wrap Pouch,
page 84*

*Sewing Machine Bag,
page 88*

# Introduction

Although I have spent my career in front of a TV camera, my hobby and my passion has always been needlecraft. For the last few years I have been fortunate to mix the two, and now my career is sewing! I love to inspire, encourage and help those new to the world of sewing to have the confidence to give it a try. The projects in this book are all simple but attractive storage solutions that you will find useful around the home. I have kept them as simple as I could, but of course more experienced sewers can adjust the sizes and embellish and decorate with appliqué or whatever stitches your machine is capable of. Enjoy making your home a tidier and more beautiful place!

Debbie x

# Useful materials and tools

**Fabric** I always use a woven cotton fabric, as I find it keeps its shape well and is easy to work with. Most of these projects use a patchwork weight, but things like the Under Bed Storage (page 50) and the Pen Case (page 58) work better with a heavier, curtain-weight fabric.

**Wadding/batting** I use 3mm (⅛in) natural wadding/batting. A heat-resistant type should be used with the Iron Caddy (page 36) and Straighteners Pouch (page 22).

**Thread** I have a box of many different colours so that I always have a matching or contrasting thread. Use a good quality, as this will be more durable and less fibrous than poor quality thread.

**Small scissors** For snipping threads and cutting into curves.

**Curved scissors** These really help when cutting out arc shapes or holes in fabric.

**Dressmaking shears** These have long blades and angled handles to make it easy to cut long lengths of fabric. Go for the best quality you can afford, as these are one of your important tools, and you will use them more often than almost anything else.

**Pinking shears** To decorate the edges of felt and to help stop woven fabric from fraying.

**Paper scissors** Keep a pair just for paper, as cutting paper can blunt your dressmaking scissors.

**Sewing machine** For the projects in this book, you don't need a top-of-the-range machine; look for one with a drop-feed facility for free motion embroidery. It should also have a range of feet included: A **walking foot** feeds the fabric through your machine from the top, along with the feed dogs underneath the fabric. It is particularly useful with multiple layers of fabric, when you are sewing different weights of fabric together or sewing fabric with a plush that could slip. A **zipper foot** takes your needle close to the teeth of a zip. You will also use it if you are putting piping into a project. For free motion embroidery, drop the feed dogs on your machine and put a **free motion embroidery foot** on to the presser foot shank, then feed the fabric through in any direction you like. The foot 'hops' over the fabric as you sew. You will need a denim needle for the Laundry Bag on page 76.

**Rotary cutter, mat and ruler** For an accurate, quick cut and to make sure corners are square, the combination of ruler, rotary cutter and mat is invaluable. I recommend a 45mm (1¾in) rotary cutter, 61 x 15cm (24 x 6in) ruler and as large a cutting mat as you have space for!

**Tape measure** A plastic tape measure will not stretch like a fabric one; buy one with both inches and centimetres if you can.

**Thimble** A must for hand sewing. I prefer a leather thimble as your needle won't slip against it.

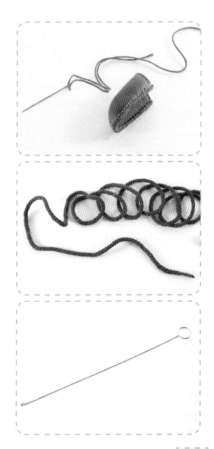

**Hand sewing needles** You'll always need these. I use sharps that have a small round head and slip through fabric easily.

**Air erasable pens** Air erasable pens contain ink that disappears after a few hours. Some pens use ink that needs to be washed out.

**Spray fabric adhesive** This holds layers of fabric together and is invaluable for appliqué. Make sure it has been manufactured specifically for fabric so that it will not damage your sewing machine.

**Cord** The cord I have used for the Laundry Bag (page 76) is just 0.5cm (¼in) piping cord. I dyed it red for the Toy Bag (page 20).

**Loop turner** This simple tool makes it much easier to turn tubes the right side out. It threads through the tube and catches on the end, then you just pull through to turn the item out.

# Basic techniques

## Seams

The seam allowance used in this book is 6mm (¼in) unless specified. I find with craft projects this is ample, and makes the seams neater if turning. For projects like the Sewing Machine Bag (page 88), I used a 12mm (½in) seam allowance to make sure that all the threads of the fabric have been caught and the seam is strong. Most projects will require pressing, and the seams are usually pressed open. Pressing sets the stitches and smooths out the stitch line. Be careful not to apply too much pressure, as this can distort the seam.

If you have a fabric that frays readily, it may be an idea to zigzag stitch the edges before sewing the pieces together. This will help stop fraying.

## Bias binding

Bias binding gives a neat, professional finish to your projects and can be used instead of hemming. Bias tape is cut on the diagonal so it gives a little round corners and curves. You can cut your own if you need a specific colour, but this can be a bit fiddly if you don't have bias making tools.

Open out the bias binding and pin to the edge of your fabric, folding over the end of the tape by about 6mm (¼in) to make the join neat. Sew along the crease with a medium straight stitch. Fold the bias tape over the edge of the fabric and pin. When you get to the join, make sure the end of the tape is tucked inside the folded end. Hand stitch on the underside if you don't want to see the stitching, or sew all layers together from the top if you don't mind seeing it.

## Fabric bag handles

This is an easy method for making handles and straps that doesn't involve making tubes and turning, which can be tricky on long handles. Cut your fabric to the length of handle required, plus an extra 5cm (2in) to allow for hemming. For a 2.5cm (1in) wide strap, cut the fabric to 10cm (4in) wide. Fold the ends of the fabric inwards by 12mm (½in) and press (if your handles are to be sewn into the seam of a bag, skip this stage). Fold the whole strap in half lengthways and press. Open up and fold each raw edge in to the centre crease and press again. Fold in half again with the two folded edges perfectly aligned and top stitch all the way round the handle.

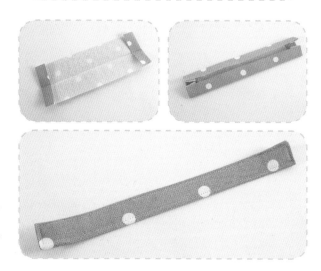

# Bag feet

If your bag or caddy is to sit on the floor, these feet will help to keep it clean, and at the same time give a professional look to your project. The feet are like large brads. You'll need to make a hole with a sharp tool where the feet are to be positioned, then push the foot through from the bottom. Open the post slightly and thread on the clip to secure from the top, then open up the post completely.

# Fitting sliders to a continuous zip

Always buy a longer zip than you need, as you will lose an inch or so at each end. It doesn't matter which end you fit the slider. You can fit two: one from each end of the zip.

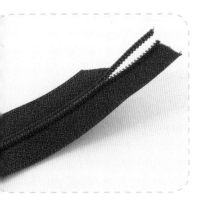

Open up the end of the zip by about 2.5cm (1in). Cut the tape away from the teeth on one side. Trim the opposite side to the same length. Pop the slider over the exposed teeth and catch the opposite side as you pull down.
Hold onto the teeth and pull. If you need two sliders on your zip, do the same at the opposite end of the tape. If the zip is uneven, with a bit of force, you can pull the two sides to bring the teeth into line.

# Eyelets

Mark on the wrong side of your fabric where the eyelet should go. Place the ring under this mark with the textured edge at the top. Place the tool in the centre and give the ring a bash with a hammer. This makes a hole in the fabric.

Turn the ring over and reposition it under the fabric, with the larger piece of the eyelet sitting on top. Place the hole in the fabric face down on top, followed by the smaller piece of the eyelet. Put the tool in the top and hammer again. Make sure your measurements are accurate, as once attached, the eyelet is permanent!

## Round petals

# Fabric flowers

These make lovely embellishments for your storage solutions, or for hair bands or clothing. For a round-petal flower, cut five circles of fabric around 7.5cm (3in) in diameter. Fold each in half and press. Sew a running stitch round the curved side of the first half-circle and pull the thread to gather. Don't break the thread, but move straight on to the next petal. When you have gathered all five, pull the thread tightly to form a circle, and hide the raw edge with a button or two.

## Pointed petals

For the pointed petals, take five circles of fabric measuring about 7.5cm (3in) in diameter, fold them in half, then into quarters, and press. Sew a running stitch round the curved edge and pull to gather. Don't break the thread, but move straight on to the next petal until you have gathered all five, then pull into a circle and secure at the centre. Sew buttons into the middle of the flower to hide the raw edge.

# Pressing

I like my steam generator iron as I can leave it on for hours, but no steam when pressing open seams as this could distort the fabric.

# Drawing a circle

When the circle you need is bigger than even your largest dinner plate, it's time to make your own compasses! Take your air erasable pen and tie a piece of string or ribbon as close as you can to the nib. Fold the fabric into quarters. From the centre of the fold, measure the radius of your circle. Place the pen on this mark, and hold the string on the corner folds. Keeping the pen upright, carefully draw an arc from one side to the other. Cut out. When you open up the fabric, you should have a perfect circle!

# Useful stitches

## Machine stitches

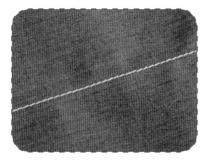

**Straight stitch**
Straight stitch is used to join fabric together, hem or top stitch.

**Zigzag stitch**
Zigzag stitch is used around hems to help stop the fabric fraying.

**Back tacking**
Whenever starting and ending a length of stitches on your sewing machine, reverse a couple of stitches to stop the row coming undone. Some machines have a locking stitch, which will put a few stitches in the same place to secure before sewing.

## Hand stitches

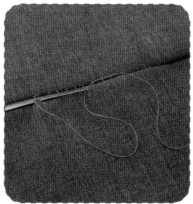

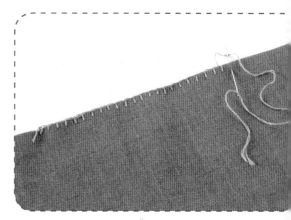

**Slip stitch**
I use this stitch to finish off bias binding. Keep the stitches small and even for the best finish.

**Ladder stitch**
This is used for closing an opening, for instance in the Hoop Basket, page 60.

**Blanket stitch**
This is not just for decoration; when the stitches are sewn very close together, they can stop fabric from fraying and make perfect buttonholes. This stitch was used on the Jewellery Pouch, page 40.

# Chair Back Caddy

Many of us have limited space for our craft supplies, so this useful storage solution makes the most of an unused area, and could easily be adapted to hang over the back of a car seat.

1 Iron the stabiliser to the back of one piece of fabric of each size, and the fusible wadding/batting to a back piece.

2 Pair the fabric pieces of the same size, wrong sides together. Put the back section to one side, and sew bias binding across the top of each of the other pieces, which will be the pockets. As this caddy will not be going in the wash, you can glue the bias binding to the back of the pockets if you prefer.

3 Using a small plate or something similar as a template, cut the corners of the back section to round them off.

**4** Take the largest pocket and place the long pocket across the front. Pin then tack/baste down each side, close to the raw edge.

**5** Fold the loose fabric into equal pleats and sew the edges of the pleats together.

**6** I stitched a strip of bias binding over the top of my handle tape as a decorative feature. Position the straps onto the back of the bag, with hook and loop fastening at each end, and sew. Measure the position of the straps against the chair to make sure they are in the right place.

**7** Turn back over, lay all the pockets in place, pin, then tack/baste all the way round, close to the edge.

**8** Sew your bias binding all the way around.

**9** Hand sew the hook and loop fastening inside the gusseted pocket to stop it gaping.

### Tip
Add a button to the centre of the bottom pocket as a divider if you wish.

# Storage Cube

These handy storage boxes will keep you organised in the craft room, kitchen or kids' rooms. They are made with squares of fabric; I used five each of two contrasting fabrics. You can make them to match your décor and personalise them with names and labels if you wish!

## What you need

For each cube, ten 25.5cm (10in) squares of fabric

Four strips of fabric for handles measuring 10 x 20.5cm (4 x 8in)

Ten 23cm (9in) squares of medium-weight, single-sided fusible stiffener

Spray fabric adhesive

**1** Iron the stiffener centrally to the wrong side of the outer fabric. Make fabric bag handles as in the instructions on page 10.

**2** Sew the sides of four outer pieces of fabric together with a 12mm (½in) seam allowance to make a tube.

3  Pin the base square in place and sew all the way round.

4  Do the same with the lining fabric.

5  Drop the lining into the outer cube. Fold the tops of the lining and outer cubes inwards towards each other by 12mm (½in). Pin them, attaching the handles on opposite sides by pinning in between the lining and the outer fabric. Sew all the way round the top.

## Tip

To personalise a cube, print a photograph on printable canvas and apply it to the side of the cube. Some printable fabric is fusible so is ironed on. I chose a loose-weave canvas as I wanted to fray the edge. This dog food cube was made in the same way as the pretty fabric ones, but I used hessian instead of cotton.

# Toy Bag

What an easy way to store soft toys or play bricks, and this useful bag doubles up as a play mat!

### *What you need*

A circle of outer fabric measuring 66cm (26in) in diameter

A circle of lining fabric measuring the same

Two 114cm (45in) lengths of 6mm (¼in) cord (mine is dyed red)

Four 12mm (½in) metal eyelets

**1** Draw and cut out your circles using the Drawing a circle technique on page 10. Fold the outer fabric circle in half and mark the edges on the fold line. Measure 3.3cm (1½in) from the raw edge and draw two dots, 3.3cm (1½in) apart. Do the same at the opposite side of the circle. Fix an eyelet on each dot, as shown on page 11.

**2** Pin the two circles right rides together, and sew all the way around, leaving a gap of around 7.5cm (3in) for turning. Snip into the seam, turn, and press. Sew up the gap with a ladder stitch (see page 13).

**3** Sew a circle of top stitch 6mm (¼in) from the edge, then another 5cm (2in) from the edge, to make a channel for the cord.

**4** Thread one length of cord through one eyelet, all the way round the circle and out through the eyelet next to it. You may find it easier to wrap a little sticky tape around the ends of the cord to stop it fraying and pop a safety pin on the end while threading.

**5** Turn the circle round and thread the other piece of cord through the opposite eyelets and all the way round the circle as before. Knot the loose ends of the cord and pull either side to draw the bag closed.

> *Tip*
> This bag could be made much larger to hold even more toys!

# Straighteners Pouch

Store away your hair straighteners or curling irons whilst they are still warm, in this handy pouch, lined with heat-resistant fabric. There's even a pocket on the back to keep the lead tidy!

## What you need

- 25.5cm (10in) square of cotton fabric
- 25.5cm (10in) square of heat-resistant wadding/batting
- 25.5cm (10in) square of ironing board cover fabric
- A piece of fabric measuring 23 x 20.5cm (9 x 8in) for the pocket
- 13cm (5in) of 6mm (¼in) elastic
- Small safety pin
- 63.5cm (25in) of 12mm (½in) bias binding

1 Lay the ironing board fabric, shiny side down, on your cutting mat, place the wadding/batting shiny side down on top, and finally the cotton fabric facing upwards. Tack them together around the edges if you wish. Cut the top right-hand corner into a curve.

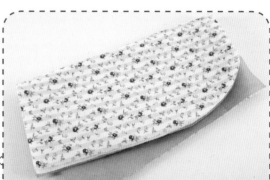

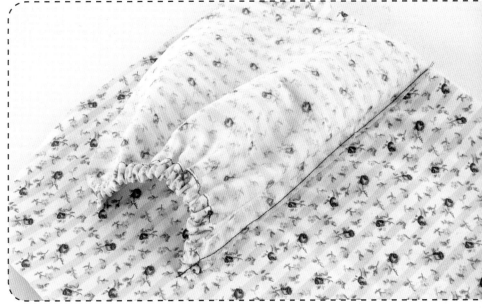

**2** Take the pocket fabric and measure 4cm (1½in) in from each bottom corner, and cut from these points to the top corners. Fold over the top twice to just over 6mm (¼in) and top stitch to make a channel for the elastic. Pop the safety pin through the end of the elastic and thread through the channel. Stitch either end to secure.

**3** Fold the main pouch in half widthways and finger press to mark, then place the pocket face down over the front half. Sew along the centre crease.

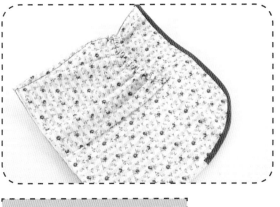

**4** Fold the pocket over and sew close to the edge along the other two sides. Apply the bias binding (see page 10) from the bottom of the curve across the top of the pouch.

**5** Fold the pouch in half again, and finish off the side and base of the pouch with bias binding.

*Tip*
Sew a loop of ribbon to the top of the pouch if you want to hang it up.

# Craft Caddy

If you're crafting on the go, this handy caddy has a pocket for all your tools, glues, pens, tapes, patterns and more! I used a heavy-weight cotton for both the outside of the caddy and the lining, as this helps to make it sturdy. You will need about 68cm (¾ yard) each of two fabrics.

## What you need

For the sides, two pieces of outer fabric measuring 40.5 x 28cm (16 x 11in)

Two pieces of lining fabric measuring the same

For the ends, two pieces of outer fabric measuring 28 x 15cm (11 x 6in) and two lining pieces measuring the same

For the pockets, four pieces of outer fabric measuring 18 x 53.5cm (7 x 21in) and four pieces of lining fabric measuring the same

For the base, one piece of outer fabric measuring 40.5 x 15cm (16 x 6in) and one piece of lining fabric measuring the same

A piece of bag base or stiff cardboard measuring 38 x 13cm (15 x 5in)

For the handles, two strips of fabric measuring 6.5 x 25.5cm (2½ x 10in)

Four buttons

Four bag feet

Two 38cm (15in) lengths of 12mm (½in) dowelling

114cm (45in) of 2.5cm (1in) bias binding

Strong fabric glue

1 Place all of the pocket pieces right sides together with their linings and sew across the top. Turn the right way and press.

**2** Take the two outer sides of the bag and pin the sides of the long pockets across the front of each.

**3** Pin the centre point and sew down the pocket to secure it, back tacking at the top end a couple of times to strengthen.

**4** Fold and crease the pleats of the pockets, making sure they are the same distance from the centre stitches, and top stitch the creases. Pin, then sew straight across the bottom.

**5** For the inside pockets, again sew each end to the right side of the lining fabric. This time, fold the pocket fabric into 'tubes' to hold pens etc. It doesn't matter if they aren't uniform in size. Pin then sew down the edges of each tube, back tacking again at the top. Sew straight across the bottom, folding all the tubes over in the same direction.

**6** Make the bag lining by sewing the sides to the ends, then pin in the base and sew.

**7** Do the same with the outside of the bag, then turn the right way out. Glue the bag base to the bottom of this outer casing. When the glue is dry, attach the bag feet at each corner of the base (see Bag feet, page 11).

**8** Drop the lining into the bag and pin the sides together.

**9** Sew the bias binding (see page 10) around the top of the caddy and fold the top over by 3cm (1½in).Make up the handles (see Fabric bag handles, page 10) and sew on to the top of each side centrally, securing with a button at each end. Insert the dowelling under the fold along each long side, and glue in place.

### Tip

You could add more pockets to the sides of the bag, and add stiffener if you need the bag to be stronger. I have decorated this caddy with one of the fabric flowers from page 12.

# Small Case

This zippered little case stores anything from knitting yarns to pens and rulers for school, or would make a useful case for musical instruments like recorders! I have used quite a heavy cotton fabric to help the case keep its shape.

## What you need

Two pieces of outer fabric measuring 40.5 x 15cm (16 x 6in) for the sides

Two pieces of lining fabric measuring the same

One piece of outer fabric measuring 40.5 x 10cm (16 x 4in) for the base

Piece of foam board or stiff card measuring 38 x 7.5cm (15 x 3in) for the inner base

Lining fabric to cover measuring 48 x 15cm (19 x 6in)

For the zipped panel, contrast fabric measuring 76 x 13cm (30 x 5in) and a strip of lining measuring the same

Continuous zip with two sliders measuring 76cm (30in)

Spray fabric adhesive

25.5cm (10in) each of ribbon and lace for a handle

Button

**1** Take the two long strips of fabric, outer and lining, and cut in half lengthways. Sew one edge of the zip face down to the outer fabric, then lay the lining on top and sew over the same stitches. Repeat with the opposite side of the zip. Press, avoiding the nylon teeth, or the iron may melt them.

**2** Place this panel, right sides together with one of the side sections. Pin then sew around three sides as shown.

**3** Place the lining fabric so that it sandwiches the zippered panel in between the two sides; pin and sew again over the same stitches. Turn the right way out.

**4** Sew the second side of the bag to the zippered section in the same way, with the outer fabric to one side of the zip and the lining to the other side. This is what the case looks like now, before the base is added.

**5** Turn the case inside out and pin then sew in the base, right sides together. Make sure the zip is open a little way to allow for turning.

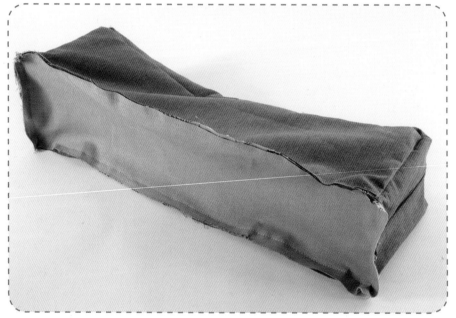

**6** Turn the case right sides out. To make the inner base, cover the cardboard with its fabric and glue to secure.

**7** When dry, put a little glue around the edge of the underside of the base, and push inside the case, being careful not to smear any glue on the lining. Tuck the raw seams in the bottom of the bag under the hard base to make it look tidy.

**8** For the handle, sew or glue the ribbon to the lace. Make a loop and attach it to a corner of the case with a button.

*Tip*
If this is intended as a school pencil case, it would be fun to personalise it with appliqué or fabric paint!

# Garment Cover

A stylish clothes protector for a jacket or blouse, with a handy pocket at the back. Measure your garment before buying the fabric and adjust the measurements if the bag needs to be longer. Mine is to fit a blazer-style jacket. I have been generous with the zip and gusset sections, but you can trim these down if you need to.

## What you need

Piece of main fabric measuring 56 x 102cm (22 x 40in)

Piece of contrasting fabric measuring 56 x 102cm (22 x 40in)

Strip of contrasting fabric measuring 23 x 102cm (9 x 40in) for the zip panel

Length of fabric for the gusset, 10cm (4in) wide and measuring 3.35m (11ft) long, or join a couple of pieces

Piece of fabric measuring 56 x 35.5cm (22 x 14in) for the pocket

6.7m (22ft) of 2.5cm (1in) bias binding

1.63m (64in) continuous zip plus two sliders

Coat hanger

Air erasable pen

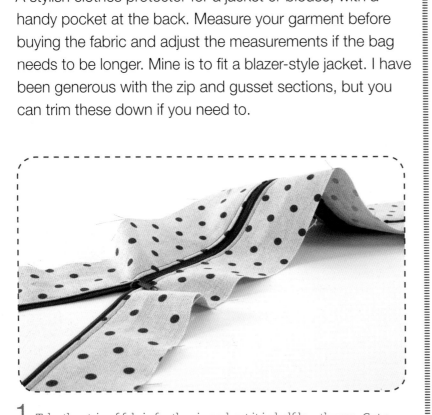

1 Take the strip of fabric for the zip and cut it in half lengthways. Cut a 76cm (30in) length off the continuous zip and attach a slider. Pin the zip right sides together with the long edge of the fabric and sew. You will need a zipper foot for this. Do the same with the opposite side of the zip and the other half of the strip of fabric.

2 Cut the main fabric in half lengthways and pin then sew in the zip panel. I also top stitched along the side of the zip to add a bit more stability.

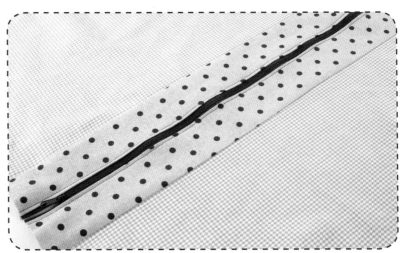

**3** Take the contrasting back fabric and cut a straight line across, 28cm (11in) from the bottom. This will make the pocket on the back of the bag. Insert the rest of the zip with the slider.

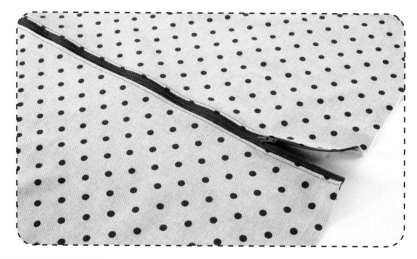

**4** Take the pocket fabric and lay it face down over the back of the pocket zip so that the right side will show through when the zip is open.

**5** Fold back towards the top of the bag and sew across the top, so that you don't see the raw edge when you fold it back into position.

**6** Fold to the first position again and pin across the bottom to hold it in place.

**7** Place the coat hanger centrally at the top of the bag, and draw around one half with an air erasable pen.

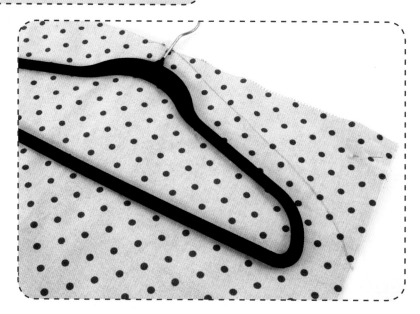

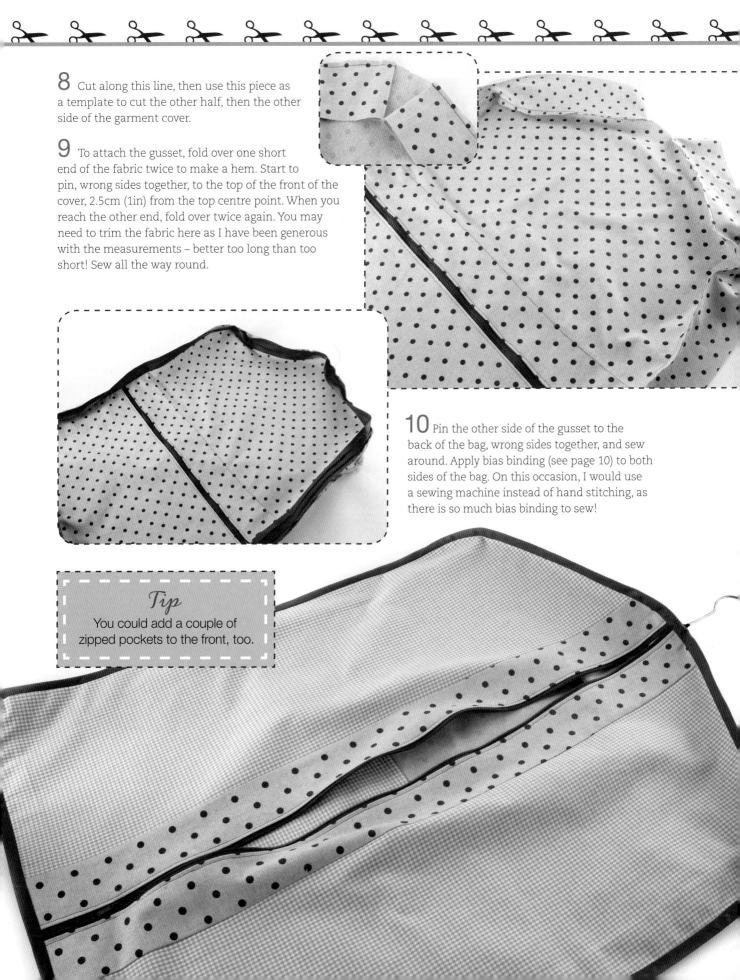

**8** Cut along this line, then use this piece as a template to cut the other half, then the other side of the garment cover.

**9** To attach the gusset, fold over one short end of the fabric twice to make a hem. Start to pin, wrong sides together, to the top of the front of the cover, 2.5cm (1in) from the top centre point. When you reach the other end, fold over twice again. You may need to trim the fabric here as I have been generous with the measurements – better too long than too short! Sew all the way round.

**10** Pin the other side of the gusset to the back of the bag, wrong sides together, and sew around. Apply bias binding (see page 10) to both sides of the bag. On this occasion, I would use a sewing machine instead of hand stitching, as there is so much bias binding to sew!

*Tip*
You could add a couple of zipped pockets to the front, too.

# Iron Caddy

This cute travel-iron holder opens out into a mini ironing surface, so if you are short of space, or going on holiday, it is perfect for you! Please be aware that although the wadding/batting is heat-resistant, it is not entirely heat-proof, so be careful of the surface on which you place it.

## What you need

Piece of fabric measuring 56 x 71cm (22 x 28in)

Piece of heat-resistant wadding/batting measuring the same

Piece of ironing board fabric measuring the same

Two 30.5cm (12in) strips of tape for the handles (I used hessian webbing to complement my fabric; you could use ribbon or fabric)

Two buttons

Two 7.5cm (3in) strips of 6mm (¼in) elastic

Pencil

Air erasable pen

1 Lay out the ironing board fabric and mark a line 20.5cm (8in) in from each edge. You will see a rectangle shape in the centre of the fabric. Use a pencil so that you can rub out the marks. Draw a diagonal line from each corner of the rectangle to a point on the edge of the fabric, 5cm (2in) in from the original lines.

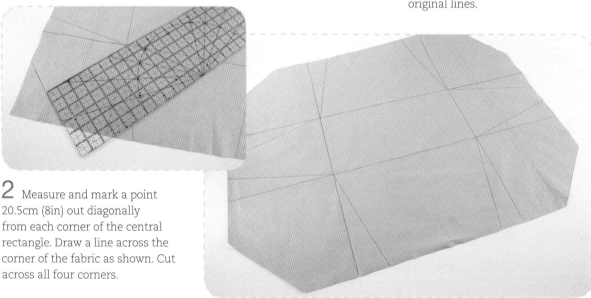

2 Measure and mark a point 20.5cm (8in) out diagonally from each corner of the central rectangle. Draw a line across the corner of the fabric as shown. Cut across all four corners.

**3** Iron the heat-resistant wadding/batting to the wrong side of the main fabric. Place the ironing board fabric on top and pin together. Cut across the corners of the fabric so that all three layers are the same size. Stitch around the central rectangle using your walking foot and a long stitch, then sew outwards along the eight diagonal lines as shown.

**4** Fold the caddy into this shape and pin.

**5** Use air erasable pen to put a mark where the elastic fastening and button should go. Do this on both sides, and attach the elastic pieces with pins, facing inwards.

**6** Lay the caddy out flat and pin the handles in position.

**7** Sew the bias binding (see page 10) all the way round the raw edges, making sure you sew a couple of times over the handles and elastic to make them secure.

**8** Finally, hand-sew on the buttons.

*Tip*
Try increasing the dimensions to hold a full-sized iron.

# Jewellery Pouch

This is a pretty presentation pouch if you are giving some jewellery as a gift, but it is also useful to take on your travels, to prevent your precious metals from getting scratched.

## What you need

Two circles of outer fabric measuring 28cm (11in) in diameter

Two circles of pocket fabric measuring 19cm (7½in) in diameter

Circle of card measuring 6.5cm (2½in) in diameter

102cm (40in) of ribbon

Safety pin

Spray fabric adhesive

Air erasable pen

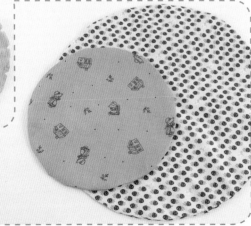

**1** Place the two sets of circles right sides together and sew all around the edge with a 6mm (¼in) seam allowance. Snip into the seam to make them neater when turned.

**2** Make a small central hole in one side of each circle. Turn through this hole and press.

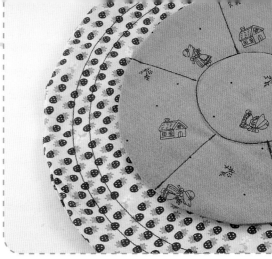

**3** Lay the outer circle hole side up, place the card circle centrally over the top and fix with a spot of glue, then fix the small circle hole side down on the top with a spot of glue.

**4** Trace around the shape of the card with the air erasable pen, and draw six lines from this central circle, evenly, to the edge of the pocket circle. Stitch over these lines to form the pockets.

**5** Sew two parallel lines, 6mm (¼in) apart, 12mm (½in) from the edge of the large circle. This makes the channel for the drawstring ribbon.

**6** With a small pair of scissors, snip a little hole into the outside of this channel to feed the ribbon through. You could blanket stitch around this hole if you prefer.

**7** Pop the safety pin on one end of the ribbon and thread through the channel.

*Tip*

A few pouches in different colours would make a pretty display, and don't just think jewellery; these little pouches are great for storing bobbins!

# Garden Tote

The green-fingered gardener will find this a useful storage tote for keeping seeds, small garden tools and gloves. You could easily increase the size to store larger items. I used linen for my bag as it creates an earthy look.

## What you need

Nine 20.5cm (8in) squares of plain main fabric

Four pieces of contrasting fabric measuring 20.5 x 15cm (8 x 6in)

Four pieces of a second contrasting fabric measuring 20.5 x 10cm (8 x 4in)

One 20.5cm (8in) square of the second contrasting fabric for the base

2.5m (98in) of bias binding; mine has an embroidered edge

Two pieces of fabric measuring 5 x 15cm (2 x 6in), for the handles

Two 15cm (6in) lengths of 12mm (½in) contrasting ribbon

Four buttons

**1** Sew the bias binding (see page 10) to the top of each piece of contrasting fabric. These will make the pocket pieces. Lay the pocket pieces on top of four squares of main fabric as shown and pin in place. These will make the outsides of the tote.

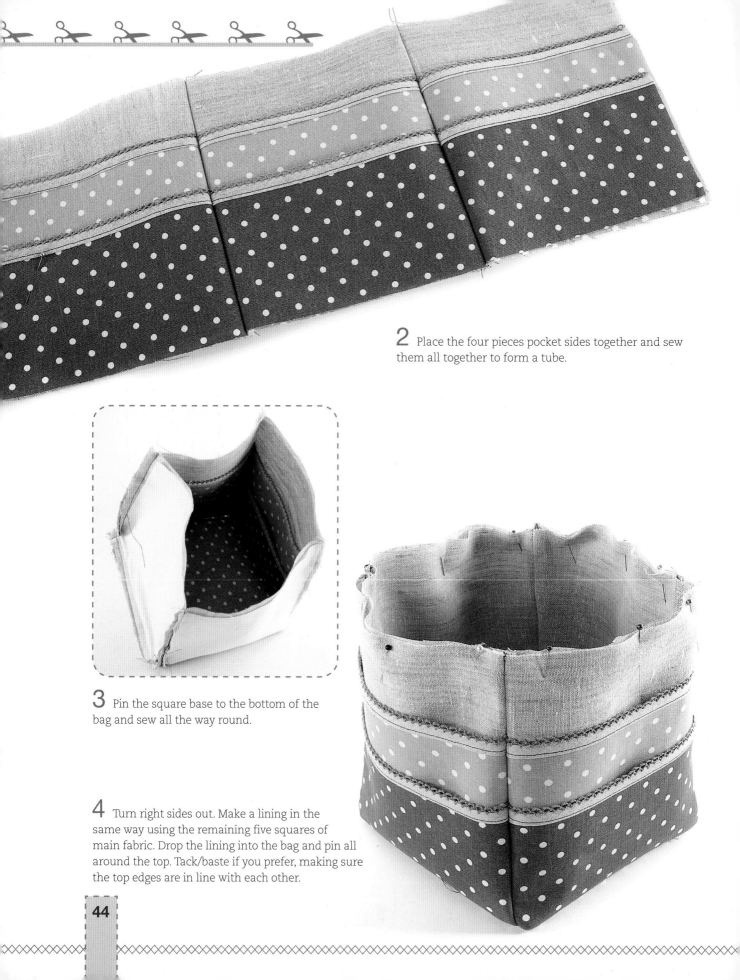

**2** Place the four pieces pocket sides together and sew them all together to form a tube.

**3** Pin the square base to the bottom of the bag and sew all the way round.

**4** Turn right sides out. Make a lining in the same way using the remaining five squares of main fabric. Drop the lining into the bag and pin all around the top. Tack/baste if you prefer, making sure the top edges are in line with each other.

**5** Apply bias binding all round the top of the tote. For the handles, fold the fabric into the centre lengthways, then stitch a piece of contrasting ribbon over the top.

**6** Pin the handles in place on either side of the tote, ends folded in, and secure with a button at each end.

### Tip

You could sew down the centre of each pocket before sewing the sides together if you wanted to make them smaller.

# Dish Carrier

A perfect way to transport hot dishes, this carrier is insulated to help keep the contents warm. Before you start, measure your casserole dish. Mine measures 23 x 15cm (9 x 6in) and is 7.5cm (3in) deep.

## What you need

One piece of outer fabric measuring 61 x 28cm (24 x 11in)

One piece of lining fabric measuring the same

One piece of insulated wadding/batting measuring the same

Two pieces of outer fabric measuring 20.5 x 28cm (8 x 11in)

Two pieces of lining fabric measuring the same

Two pieces of insulated wadding/batting measuring the same

Two 26.5cm (10½in) lengths of 12mm (¼in) dowelling

15cm (6in) of sew-in hook and loop fastening

38cm (15in) of ribbon

Small wooden spoon

20.5cm (8in) plate to use as a template

Four buttons

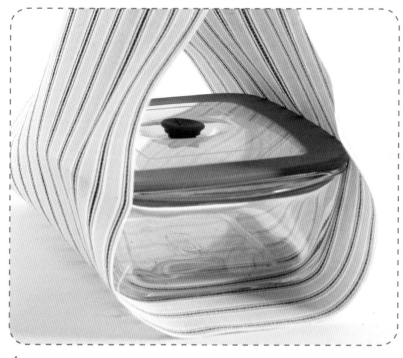

1 Wrap the long rectangle of fabric around your dish to make sure the cover is going to fit.

2 Using the plate, draw an arc on one short edge of the long rectangle of fabric and cut to make the handle. Make sure you leave 5cm (2in) either side of the arc. Take the piece you have cut out, and use this as your template to mark and cut the other end as well. Cut the same shapes from the corresponding wadding/batting and lining.

**3** Lay down the wadding/batting with the lining, right side up, on top, followed by the outer fabric right side down. Starting 20.5cm (8in) from the top, sew round the side, then the arc, and finally to 20.5cm (8in) down the second side. Repeat on the opposite end of the fabric.

**4** Snip across the corners, and into the seam allowance of the curves, then turn the right way out.

**5** Press. Where the gaps in the stitching are on each side, fold the fabrics inwards to make them sit neatly with the seams, and press again.

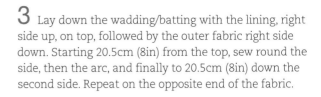

**6** For the sides, take the smaller pieces of fabric and layer them: wadding/batting first, then the lining, right side up, and finally the outer fabric right side down. Sew round three sides, leaving one short end open. Snip the corners, turn, and press. Repeat to make the other side.

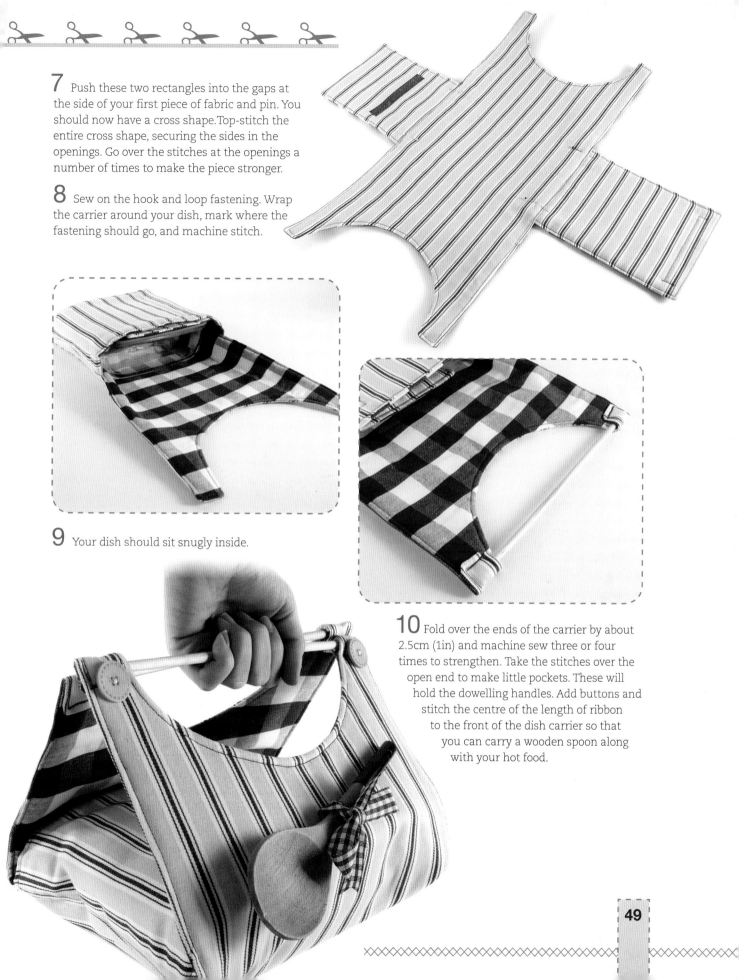

**7** Push these two rectangles into the gaps at the side of your first piece of fabric and pin. You should now have a cross shape. Top-stitch the entire cross shape, securing the sides in the openings. Go over the stitches at the openings a number of times to make the piece stronger.

**8** Sew on the hook and loop fastening. Wrap the carrier around your dish, mark where the fastening should go, and machine stitch.

**9** Your dish should sit snugly inside.

**10** Fold over the ends of the carrier by about 2.5cm (1in) and machine sew three or four times to strengthen. Take the stitches over the open end to make little pockets. These will hold the dowelling handles. Add buttons and stitch the centre of the length of ribbon to the front of the dish carrier so that you can carry a wooden spoon along with your hot food.

# Under Bed Storage

A perfect place to store sheets, knitwear or even children's toys, this zipped case keeps things neat, organised and dust free!

## *What you need*

Two pieces of fabric measuring 51 x 40.5cm (20 x 16in) for the top and bottom

Piece of iron-on stiffening measuring the same

Piece of fabric measuring 127 x 23cm (50 x 9in) for the sides

Piece of fabric measuring 46 x 24cm (18 x 9½in)

Piece of fabric measuring 25.5 x 6.5cm (10 x 2½in) for the handle

137cm (54in) continuous zip

Plate 15cm (6in) in diameter as a template

Air erasable pen

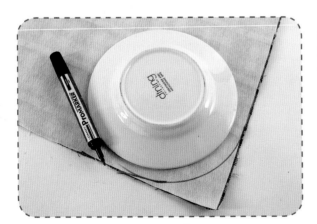

1 Iron the stiffening to the wrong side of the base piece of the case. Lay this together with the top fabric and draw an arc across each corner using a plate as a template and an air erasable pen, and cut to round off the corners (I used a marker pen for the photograph, for clarity).

2 Take the long piece of fabric for the sides and attach one side of the zip, face down, to the right side of the top edge of the fabric, using the zipper foot on your sewing machine.

**3** Fold back the zip and carefully press, avoiding the nylon teeth of the zip as they may melt!

**4** Right sides together, attach the shorter length of fabric to each end, forming a large loop.

**5** Take the lid of the case and fold in half width-wise, then mark the centre point of each side with an air erasable pen. Do the same with the zipped loop, hold the ends of the zip together to fold the loop in half and mark. Line up the centre of the loop on the zipped side with the centre of the lid and pin. Then pin all the way around, before sewing together on your machine.

**6** Repeat with the base: mark the centre points, pin to the side section and sew all the way round. Make sure the zip is open slightly for turning. Start sewing from the front of the bag, then if your fabric shifts you can take in or let out the side seams slightly for a perfect fit.

**7** Take the handle fabric, and follow the Fabric bag handles instructions on page 10. Pin the handle to the centre of the front and sew to secure.

# Nursery Bag

This handy bag for stacking nappies/diapers could hang either over the side of the cot or on a coat hanger, and is much more attractive than the usual plastic packaging.

## What you need

A piece of foam board or stiff card measuring 15 x 28cm (6 x 11in)

Fabric to cover it measuring 23 x 35.5cm (9 x 14in)

Fabric for the bag measuring 51 x 91.5cm (20 x 36in)

Two strips of fabric measuring 10 x 20.5cm (4 x 8in) for the straps

Two 5cm (2in) strips of hook and loop fastening

One 28cm (11in) piece of 6mm (¼in) dowelling

Spray fabric adhesive

Three buttons

**1** Cover the foam board with fabric, tucking the fabric to the underside, and glue in place.

**2** Fold in the ends of the strap fabric and press, then fold the sides into the centre, then fold in half again and press. Place one side of the hook and loop fastening on the end, then stitch all the way round. Repeat to make two.

**3** Fold over the shorter sides of the bag fabric twice and top stitch to hem. Fold the fabric in half, hemmed sides together, and finger crease to make the centre point, then pin the two hemmed edges to this mark.

**4** Sew straight across one edge, which will make the bottom of the nursery bag.

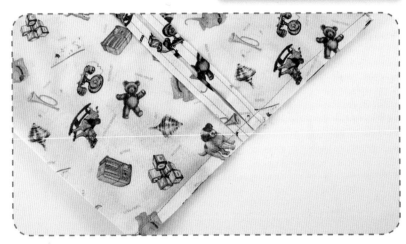

**5** At the bottom, measure 5cm (2in) in from each side, and 5cm (2in) up, then cut out the square shape on each corner. Open up the cut sections and sew across them to form the base of the bag.

**6** At the top, fold in either side by 6.5cm (2½in) and pin.

**7** At this point, insert the straps facing inwards, hook and loop ends first, at an equal distance from the edge, and stitch across the seam.

**8** Turn the right way round, fold over the straps to see where to position the other half of the hook and loop fastening, and sew in place. Add buttons to decorate.

**9** Insert the base into the bottom of the bag. Hand-stitch the opening with a ladder stitch, to around 10cm (4in) up the front of the opening. I popped a button on at this point to help strengthen the seam.

**10** Run a little glue across the dowelling and fit it across the inside of the top of the bag. Hang the nursery bag over the side of the cot/crib, or on a coat hanger.

*This useful bag also doubles as a handy storage solution for your bathroom.*

# Knitting Needle Roll

Pair up your needles in this double-pocketed knitting roll, and there's a place for your row counters too!

## What you need

Outer fabric measuring 25.5 x 51cm (10 x 20in)

Lining fabric measuring the same

Two pieces of fabric for the large pocket measuring 25.5 x 20.5cm (10 x 8in)

Two pieces for the smaller pocket measuring 25.5 x 15cm (10 x 6in)

2.44m (8ft) of 2.5cm (1in) bias binding

Button

Plate for template

1 Sew bias binding across the top of the two pockets, in each case joining the two fabrics. Lay the lining fabric on top of the outer fabric to form the roll, with the pockets on top. Cut the top two corners of the roll into an arc using a small plate as a template.

56

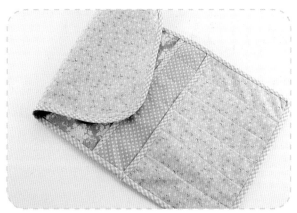

**2** Divide the pockets into six sections by stitching five lines down them as shown, back tacking at the top of each pocket to secure. Pin bias binding all the way round the outside of the roll.

**3** Sew the bias binding in place (see page 10). I hand stitched the back as I think it looks neater.

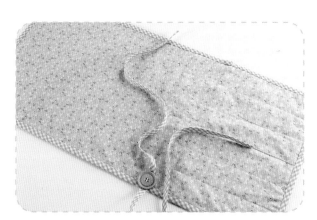

**4** Press the rest of the bias binding in half lengthways, and sew down the open edge, folding in the ends, to make a tie for the roll. Attach this to one side of the back of the roll with the button. This should be in line with the top of the pockets.

**5** And roll!

*Tip*

This roll could easily be adapted for crochet hooks, and why not try making it in denim?

# Pen Case

This is a large pen case that can also be used for storing dressing table items.

## What you need

Piece of outer fabric measuring 46 x 15cm (18 x 6in)

Piece of lining fabric measuring the same

Piece of medium-weight fusible stabiliser measuring the same

Piece of outer fabric measuring 46 x 7.5cm (18 x 3in)

Piece of lining fabric measuring the same

Piece of fusible stabiliser measuring the same

48cm (19in) nylon zip

Four circles of stabiliser measuring 14cm (5½in) across

Two circles of outer fabric measuring 16.5cm (6½in) across

Two circles of lining fabric measuring the same

Strip of fabric measuring 10 x 6.5cm (4 x 2½in) for the handle

25.5cm (10in) bias binding

Spray fabric adhesive and paper clips

1 Iron the fusible stabiliser to the back of the coordinating outer fabric rectangles.

2 Place the zip face down on the right side of the larger rectangle, then sandwich it with the lining. Pin or tack/baste it in place, fit your zipper foot and sew.

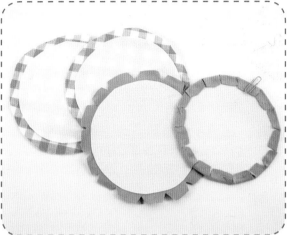

**3** Attach the zip to the smaller rectangle in the same way. Press, avoiding the nylon teeth, as they may melt. Form a tube shape, lining side out, with the ends of the zip meeting, and sew. To neaten this seam, apply the bias binding.

**4** Iron the circles of fusible stabiliser to the wrong sides of the circles of fabric. Snip into the edge of the lining circles, glue and fold over. Hold in place with a few paper clips if your glue doesn't dry quickly.

**5** Pin the outer circles into each end of the tube and sew, using your zipper foot. Fold the bias binding over the raw edge of the seam and sew to make it neat. Make sure the zip is open so that you can turn the case the right way out!

### Tip
Don't use stabiliser that is too stiff or it will be difficult to sew the circles into the tube and turn out.

**6** Glue the back of the lining circles and push them into the base and lid. Make a fabric bag handle as shown on page 10 and sew it on top of the lid.

# Hoop Basket

The wooden embroidery hoop helps to keep the shape of this useful basket. You could hang several on a rail in the kitchen, workroom, bedroom or bathroom. Smaller baskets could hold jewellery and larger ones could store balls of yarn.

## What you need

For one basket:

One 15cm (6in) wooden or bamboo embroidery hoop

Piece of outer fabric measuring 47 x 25.5cm (18½ x 10in)

Piece of lining fabric measuring the same

30.5cm (12in) of ribbon to hang

51cm (20in) ric-rac or ribbon to decorate the hoop

Spray fabric adhesive

**1** Sew the top of the outer fabric to the the top of the lining and press.

**2** Fold in half as shown, right sides together, and sew straight down the side to form a tube.

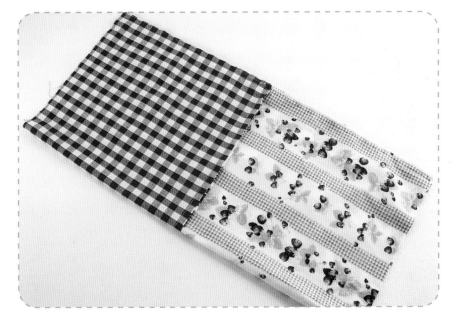

**3** Open up this tube and flatten so that the side seam is in the centre, then pin across the bottom, and sew with a 6mm (¼in) seam allowance.

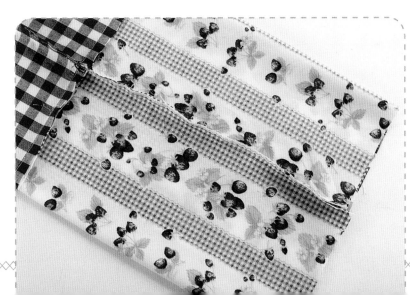

**4** Sew across the open end of the lining but leave a gap of around 7.5cm (3in) for turning. Press. Pinch all four corners, one at a time, and fold flat so that the side seam lays on top of the base seam. You should feel when they are in line with your fingers. Pin in place.

**5** Take a line straight across this corner 4cm (1½in) from the point, and sew. This will form the boxed base shape. Cut off the excess fabric. Turn the bag the right way round by pulling through the gap at the bottom of the lining. Hand-sew the opening together with a ladder stitch (see page 13).

**6** Unscrew the embroidery hoop to widen it as far as it will go. Place the inner hoop over the top of the fabric basket. Fold the fabric over the hoop by about 2.5cm (1in).

**7** Place the larger hoop over the top of the fabric-covered inner hoop with the screw at the back, and tighten the screw to secure it.

**8** Tie a ribbon to the screw at the back and you can hang up the hoop basket, tying the ribbon in a bow. Glue ric-rac or ribbon to the hoop to decorate it.

*Tip*
I have made three hoop baskets and tied them to a pole. You could fill them with dried flowers for decoration, or use them for storage.

# Drawer Liner

Although these drawer liners look pretty, they serve a practical purpose too, as they help to keep the drawer's contents in separate compartments, and can prevent delicate things from being damaged. I have made each panel separately as I want the box to be sturdy enough to lift out and use as stand-alone storage. This method tucks the fabric into the corner seams to give a really neat finish.

## What you need

For the size of my drawer, I needed 91cm (a yard) of fabric for each liner; or four fat quarters of contrasting patterns

46cm (half a yard) of 3mm (⅛in) wadding/batting

Large corrugated card box

Spray fabric adhesive

Tape measure

Air erasable pen

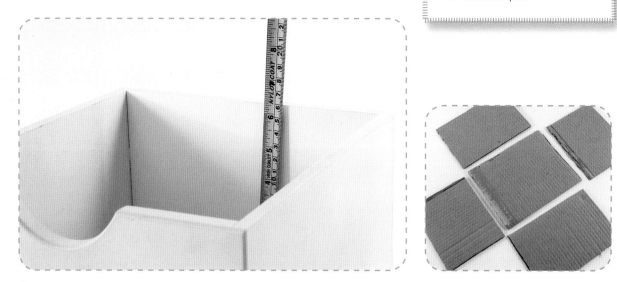

**1** Measure the inside of your drawer. Mine measures 21.5 x 24cm (8½ x 9½in) by 15cm (6in) deep.

**2** Cut your cardboard to 2.5cm (1in) less on the width and 12mm (½in) less on the depth. My base is 19 x 21.5cm (7½ x 8½in); the long sides are 21.5 x 14cm (8½ by 5½in), and the short sides are 19 x 14cm (7½ x 5½in).

**3** Cut one piece of wadding/batting for each panel, and glue to one side.

**4** Cut two pieces of fabric for each panel, adding a 2.5cm (1in) border, so that's an additional 5cm (2in) on the width and length of each piece.

**5** Place the pairs of fabric panels right sides together, and sew round three sides, leaving the bottom open, to make a sleeve for the card to slip into. Use a 6mm (¼in) seam allowance. Turn each sleeve the right way round and press.

**6** Insert the card panels into the sleeves. The sleeves may seem too big, but don't worry. Make sure the wadding/batting will be facing the inside of the drawer liner.

**7** Fold the raw edges in, fit the zipper foot on your sewing machine and top stitch across the opening.

**8** Place the side sections against the base with the top stitched edges nearest the base. Push the card away from this edge so that you won't be sewing through it, then one by one machine stitch the panels to the base. When the sides are folded up, the stitching will disappear into the folds.

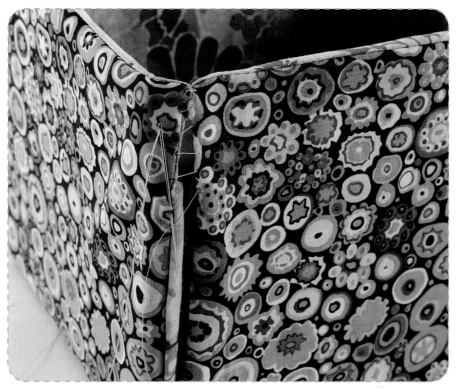

**9** Lift up the sides one by one, and hand-sew the corners with a ladder stitch (see page 13).

**10** Place this liner into the drawer, then measure the inside of the liner. Mine measures 20.5 x 23cm (8 x 9in) by 14.5cm (5¾in) deep.

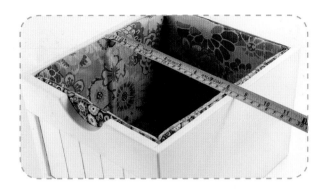

**11** For each divider, cut one piece of cardboard to the length of the liner minus 6mm (¼in), and 2.5cm (1in) less in depth. Make two. Mine measure 22 x 12cm (8¾ x 4¾in). Fold to crease in the middle.

**12** Cut four pieces of wadding/batting to the same size, and cover both sides of each divider. Cut two pieces of fabric for each divider, 12mm (½in) longer than the panel, and 2.5cm (1in) deeper. Place the two pieces right sides together, sew round the three top sides, turn out and press.

**13** Insert the card dividers into the sleeves, fold in the raw edge and sew, as with the side panels of the box. Place the dividers into the drawer liner, and secure with a little spray fabric adhesive.

*Tip*
You can make as many dividers as you wish, subdividing the ones shown here. Smaller ones could be used for jewellery and larger ones for socks.

# Toy Hammock

Create a stylish storage hammock for the nursery to keep teddies tidy! This could also be hung from a couple of hooks on the back of a door.

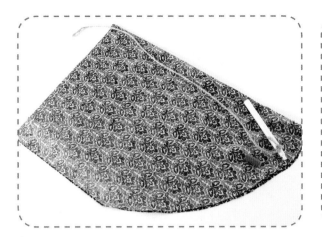

**1** Fold a main fabric piece in half widthways. Take your pen tied to string (see Drawing a circle, page 12) and hold it in the top centre corner. Draw an arc over the opposite corner, and cut out. Repeat for all four pieces of fabric.

**2** To shape the top of each fabric piece into a curve, fold the fabric in half, mark 7.5cm (3in) along the fold and 5cm (2in) from the opposite corner. Join the two marks by eye to make a curve, and cut.

**3** Lay one outer fabric piece right sides together with a lining piece and sew across the top. Repeat with the other two pieces of fabric.

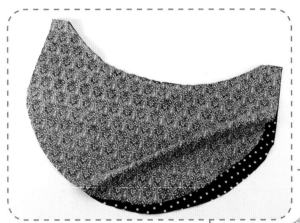

**4** Open both sides out into circles and place right sides together, making sure the seams match. Sew all the way round, leaving a gap in the lining of around 10cm (4in) for turning.

**5** Turn the right way out, and close the opening with a ladder stitch (see page 13). Push the lining into the bag and press. Attach the eyelets at the top of the hammock for the ties (see page 11).

**6** For the ties, fold the long strips of fabric in half lengthways, right sides together. Pin. Cut across each end at a 45 degree angle. Sew all the way round, leaving a gap about half way down the side for turning.

**7** Snip across the points, then use the loop turner to turn the right way out. Press, and close the gap with a ladder stitch (see page 13). Thread the ties through the eyelets and tie in bows.

**Tip**
Instead of making ties, you could use a wide ribbon instead.

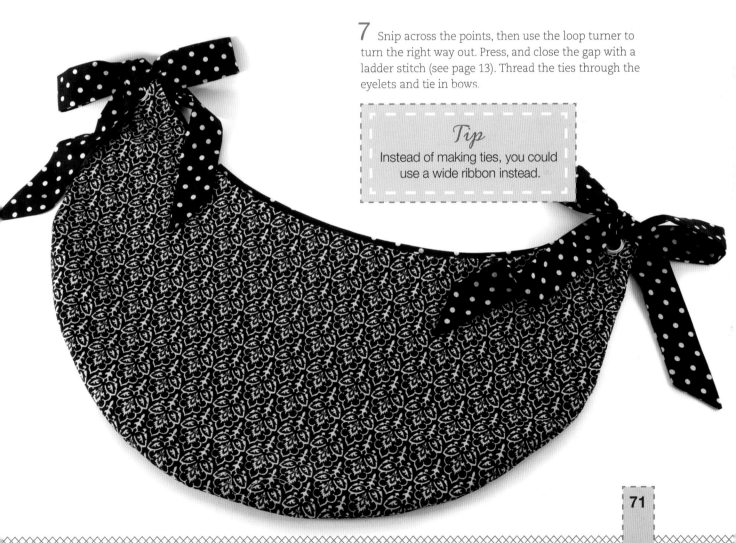

# Big Basket

You can tidy away toys, fabric or towels in this basket, or use it for laundry. Using stiffener makes the fabric quite heavy, so you'll need a denim needle in your sewing machine, and I glued on the bias binding as it became too thick to fit under the presser foot. I used a heavier weight fabric for the outside, as this helps to keep the shape, and a cotton lining fabric inside.

**1** Sandwich the stiffener between the outer and lining fabric and iron to adhere. Make sure the fabrics are smooth and flat as you iron. Repeat for the other side of the basket.

**2** Using the plate as your template, draw a curve at the two top corners and then cut the curve. Do this for both sides of the basket.

**3** For the handle, draw round the cup twice on a piece of paper and join the two circles with straight lines to create an oval template. Place this in the top centre of the basket, draw round it and cut out the shape. Curved scissors will help here. Repeat for the other side of the basket.

**4** Take the strip of bias binding and press in half lengthways. Put a little glue round one side of the handle hole and apply the bias binding. Allow this to dry, then glue to the other side. Do this for both handles.

**5** Using the same technique, glue the bias binding across the top of each side of the basket and around 10cm (4in) down each side.

**6** Machine stitch with a long stitch down each side of the basket, from the 10cm (4in) mark where the bias binding ends. Your walking foot will be helpful here. Pin the circular base of the basket in place. This is easier if you put some stuffing or something similar inside the basket to keep the shape.

**7** Sew round with your sewing machine. The basket is now quite large, so take your time to manoeuvre it under the needle!

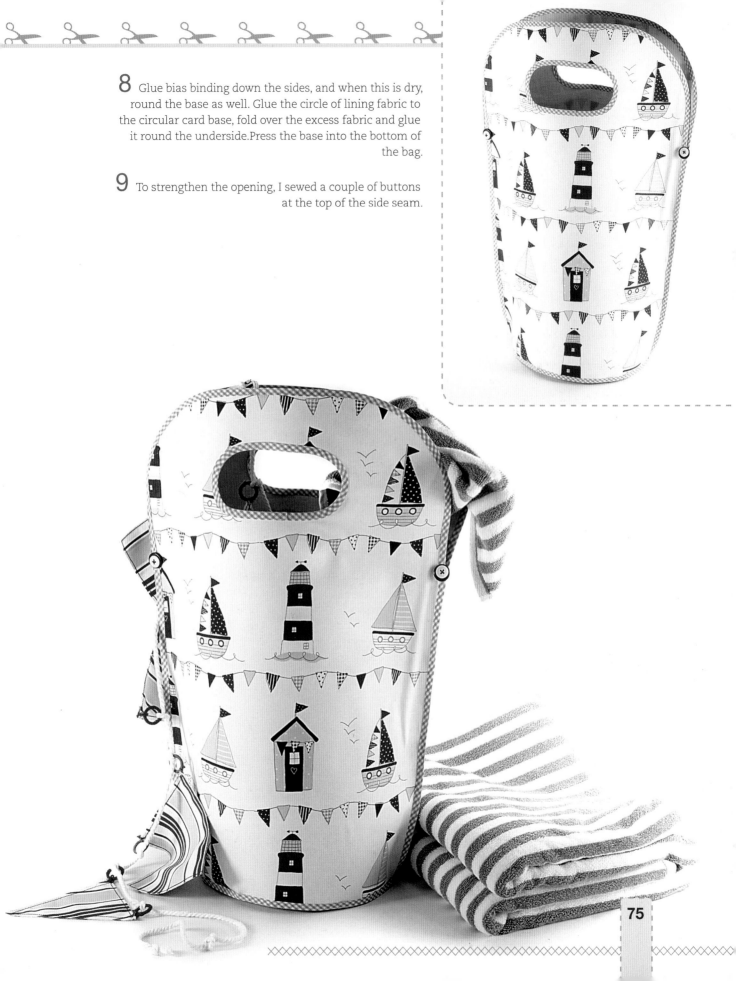

**8** Glue bias binding down the sides, and when this is dry, round the base as well. Glue the circle of lining fabric to the circular card base, fold over the excess fabric and glue it round the underside. Press the base into the bottom of the bag.

**9** To strengthen the opening, I sewed a couple of buttons at the top of the side seam.

# Laundry Bag

A fun laundry bag like this might even encourage the kids not to drop their dirty clothes on the floor! You could make one in white and one in blue for the white and coloured washes. My bag has washing line appliqué stitched on with free motion embroidery, but you could use a satin stitch on your sewing machine for the clothes and a straight stitch for the line.

## What you need

Piece of cotton fabric measuring 102 x 76cm (40 x 30in)

117cm (46in) of cord for the drawstring

Scraps of coloured fabric for the appliqué

Spray fabric adhesive

Large safety pin

**1** Cut out little shapes for clothes from the scraps of fabric. They should measure around 7.5cm (3in) high.

**2** Spray the backs of them with the glue, and position across the fabric.

**3** Put a little mark on each of the shorter sides of the fabric, about 20.5cm (8in) from the top. Drop the feed dogs on your sewing machine and use the free motion embroidery foot to stitch a washing line across the tops of the garments, beginning and ending at your marks. Go over the line a couple of times to make the stitching stand out. Sew round each of the garments to hold them in place, and stitch pegs too.

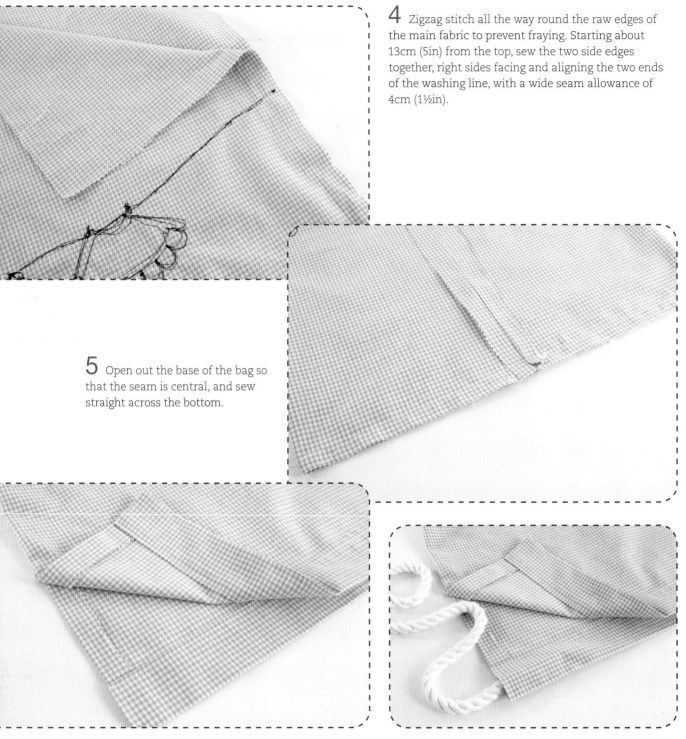

**4** Zigzag stitch all the way round the raw edges of the main fabric to prevent fraying. Starting about 13cm (5in) from the top, sew the two side edges together, right sides facing and aligning the two ends of the washing line, with a wide seam allowance of 4cm (1½in).

**5** Open out the base of the bag so that the seam is central, and sew straight across the bottom.

**6** Fold over the top edge of the fabric twice to make a hem around 2.5cm (1in) deep. Top stitch the hem.

**7** Turn the right way round and press. Place the safety pin on the end of the cord and thread through the top hem. Tie the two ends together.

Tip
You could make slightly smaller
versions of this bag to store shoes in.

# Needlecraft Booklet

This would make a lovely gift for someone who sews. Fill it with needles, pins, scissors and other sewing bits and bobs.

## What you need

Piece of outer fabric measuring 21.5 x 43cm (8½ x 17in)

Two pieces of contrast fabric 1 measuring 15 x 21.5cm (6 x 8½in) for the inside

Piece of contrast fabric 1 measuring 10 x 7.5cm (4 x 3in) for the scissor pocket

Piece of contrast fabric 2 measuring 15 x 21.5cm (6 x 8½in)

Piece of contrast fabric 2 measuring 10 x 21.5cm (4 x 8½in) for the pocket

20.5cm (8in) of 0.5cm (¼in) wide ribbon

Two 9cm (3½in) squares of felt

Piece of 3mm (⅛in) wadding/batting measuring 20.5 x 42cm (8 x 16½in)

Handful of buttons

Air erasable pen

12mm (½in) of hook and loop fastening

Spray fabric adhesive

**1** Spray the wadding/batting with glue and lay on the reverse side of the long piece of fabric centrally; you should have a 6mm (¼in) gap all the way round. Draw a heart on the right-hand third of the fabric with air erasable pen. Hand-sew the buttons in the heart shape.

**2** Sew together the contrast fabrics for the inside along the long edge, with fabric 2 in between two pieces of fabric 1. Use a 6mm (¼in) seam allowance.

**3** Take the small rectangle of contrast fabric 1, fold over one of the shorter sides by 3mm (⅛in) and top stitch. Mark a line from each of the two top corners to the bottom, 2.5cm (1in) in from each side. Press the fabric inwards along these lines.

**4** Fold the bottom edge up by 6mm (¼in) and press. This is the little scissor pocket. Place it sideways in the centre panel of the booklet and sew round three sides, leaving the top open.

**5** Arrange the two felt squares underneath the scissor pocket to look like pages, and sew down one side to secure. Hand-sew a running stitch around the edge to decorate if you wish, and felt works well when trimmed with pinking shears to give a decorative effect. Sew the middle of the little piece of ribbon in the middle of the opening of the scissor pocket. This will stop the scissors from falling out.

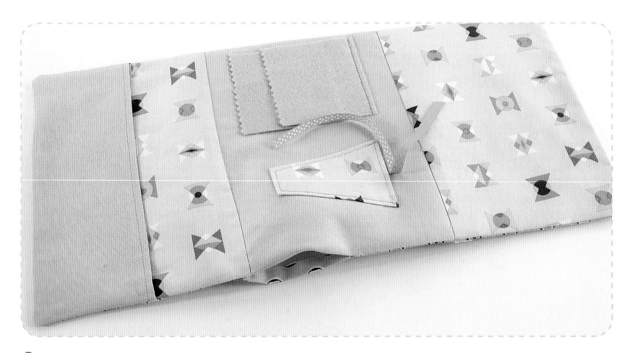

**6** Fold over the long edge of the smaller piece of contrast fabric 2 and hem it. Place this over one end of the booklet and tack/baste very close to the edge.

**7** Place the whole of this section right sides together with the long strip of fabric, and sew all the way round, leaving a gap of 5cm (2in) for turning. Turn the right way out and sew the opening closed with a ladder stitch (see page 13).

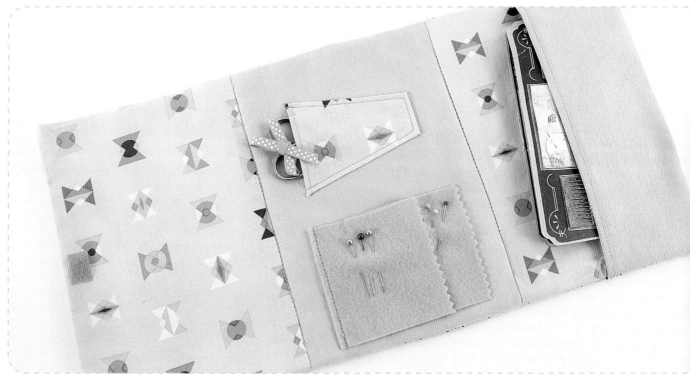

**8** Hand-sew the hook and loop fastening in place to close.

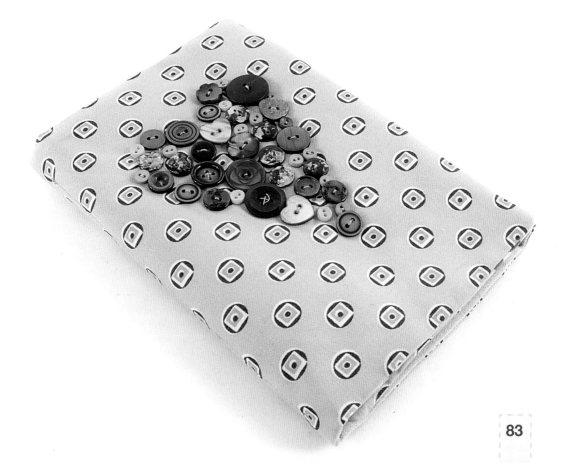

# Gift Wrap Pouch

This pouch is similar to the Hoop Baskets, but larger and longer, with pockets to store gift tags and ribbon.

## What you need

20.5cm (8in) wooden embroidery hoop

Piece of outer fabric measuring 46 x 66cm (18 x 26in)

Piece of lining fabric measuring the same

Piece of fabric measuring 66 x 25.5cm (26 x 10in) and strip of contrasting fabric measuring 66 x 15cm (26 x 6in) for the pockets

135cm (53in) bias binding

66cm (26in) of ribbon to decorate

30.5cm (12in) of ribbon to hang

Spray fabric adhesive

**1** Attach bias binding to a long edge of each pocket piece. Lay the two pockets on top of the outer bag fabric and pin, then sew in place.

**2** Machine sew in vertical lines at intervals of about 10cm (4in) to make the pockets, back tacking at the top of each pocket to secure. These pockets can vary in size depending on what you want to keep in them.

**3** Right sides together, sew the top of the fabric to the top of the lining.

**4** Fold so that the long edges meet, and sew along this edge to make a tube. Flatten out the tube so that the seam is in the centre, and stitch across the base of the bag.

**5** Open out the base of the bag into a square, and pin.

**6** Measure 4cm (1½in) from each end of the bottom seam and sew across, before cutting off the excess fabric.

**7** Do the same with the lining section, but leave a gap in the centre for turning. Turn right sides out and sew the opening closed with a ladder stitch (see page 13). Push the lining into the bag and press.

**8** Feed the top of the bag through the smaller part of the embroidery hoop and fold it over. Place the larger hoop over the top, screw to the back, and tighten. Glue a piece of ribbon round the hoop to decorate. The hanging ribbon can be tied through the screw hole at the back of the bag.

*Tip*

Why not keep scissors and sticky tape in the pockets, especially if you can never find them when there's a gift to wrap!

# Sewing Machine Bag

Sewing machine bags tend to be black or navy and a bit dull, so why not make your own in a fabric you like? I used quite a heavy woven cotton in two patterns, and canvas as thick as I could sew through! The size will fit a standard size sewing machine with a bit of room to spare, and you could adapt the measurements for a larger machine. I used foam board for the base which is sturdy enough but can be cut through. You can buy this from craft shops.

## What you need

Two pieces of heavy cotton fabric measuring 43 x 35.5cm (17 x 14in), for the front and back

Two pieces of canvas to line, measuring the same

Two pieces of fusible adhesive, measuring the same

For the zipped section, one length of fabric measuring 117 x 20.5cm (46 x 8in); this should be generous

One length of lining fabric measuring the same

Piece of fabric measuring 51 x 25.5cm (20 x 10in) for the hard inner base

Foam board measuring 40.5 x 18cm (16 x 7in) for the hard inner base

Spray fabric adhesive

117cm (46in) continuous zip with two sliders meeting in the middle

Four bag feet

229cm (90in) canvas webbing for the handles

Saucer to use as a template

Piece of fabric measuring 43 x 20.5cm (17 x 8in) for the bottom of the case

Canvas and fusible adhesive measuring the same

Two 23cm (9in) squares of fabric for the pocket

23cm (9in) of lace to trim

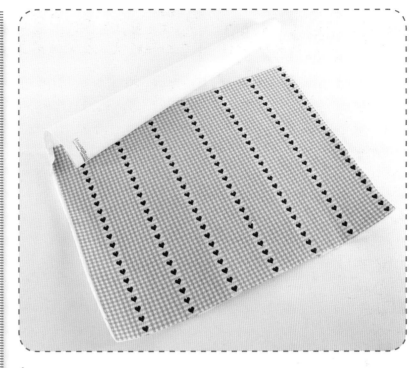

1 For the front and back, take the two rectangles of fabric measuring 43 x 35.5cm (17 x 14in), and two of the same size in canvas. Apply fusible adhesive with a hot iron to each piece of canvas, peel off the backing and re-iron on to the wrong side of your fabric.

2 Using a saucer as a template, round off the top two corners of each rectangle.

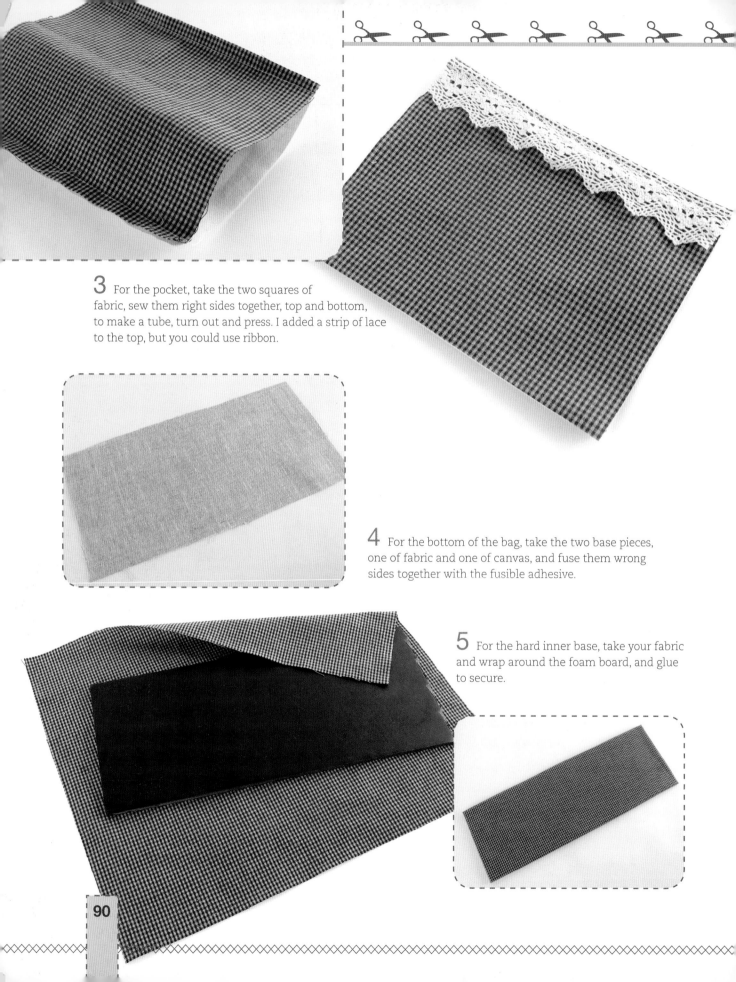

**3** For the pocket, take the two squares of fabric, sew them right sides together, top and bottom, to make a tube, turn out and press. I added a strip of lace to the top, but you could use ribbon.

**4** For the bottom of the bag, take the two base pieces, one of fabric and one of canvas, and fuse them wrong sides together with the fusible adhesive.

**5** For the hard inner base, take your fabric and wrap around the foam board, and glue to secure.

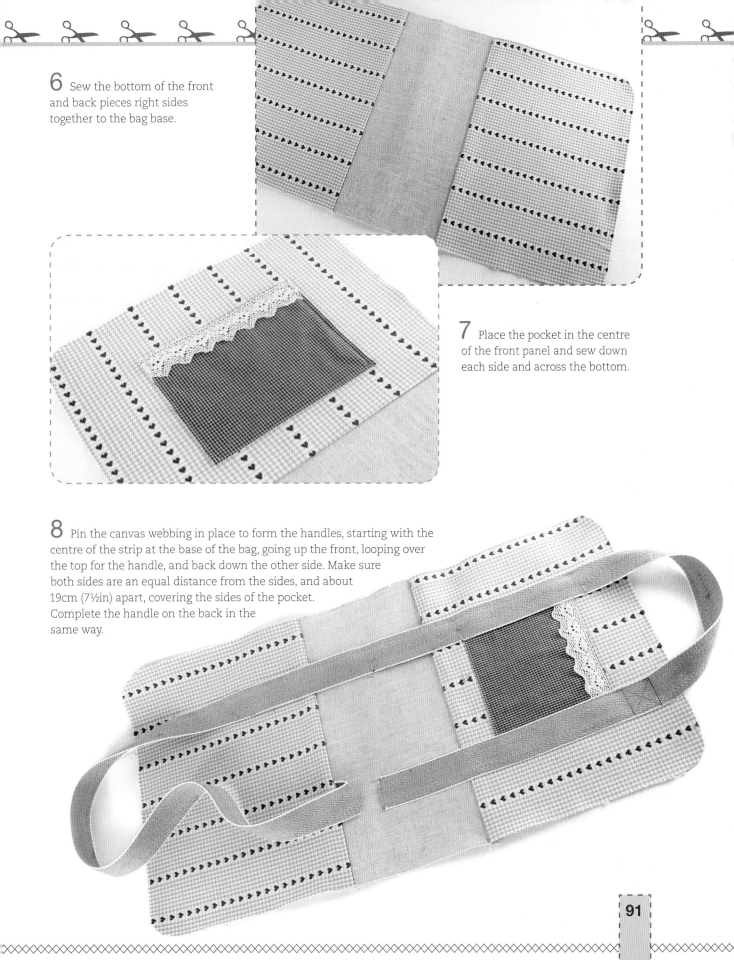

**6** Sew the bottom of the front and back pieces right sides together to the bag base.

**7** Place the pocket in the centre of the front panel and sew down each side and across the bottom.

**8** Pin the canvas webbing in place to form the handles, starting with the centre of the strip at the base of the bag, going up the front, looping over the top for the handle, and back down the other side. Make sure both sides are an equal distance from the sides, and about 19cm (7½in) apart, covering the sides of the pocket. Complete the handle on the back in the same way.

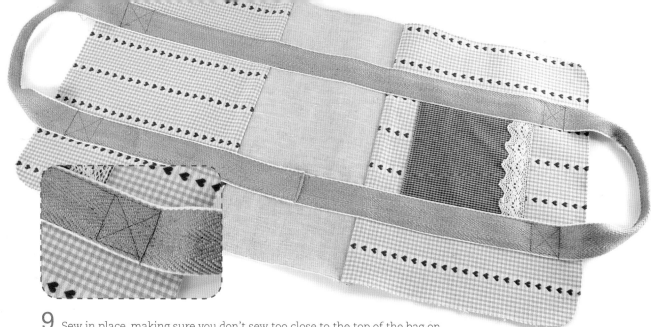

**9** Sew in place, making sure you don't sew too close to the top of the bag on either front or back, to leave room for fitting the zipped section. Sew a square with a cross inside it at the top of each side of both handles for strength.

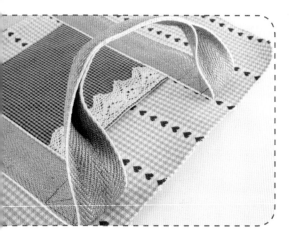

**10** Fold the handles in half where you'll hold them, then stitch together.

**11** For the zipped section, take the long strips of fabric and lining, and cut them in half lengthways.

**12** Sew the first edge of the zip face down onto a long strip of fabric. Lay the lining strip over the top and sew again. If you are confident, you can do this in one movement, sandwiching the zip between the two strips of fabric. Open up and press, then stitch the other side of the zip to the remaining two strips in the same way. Open up and press again.

**13** Sew all the way around the outside of this panel to hold its shape, and top stitch around the zipper.

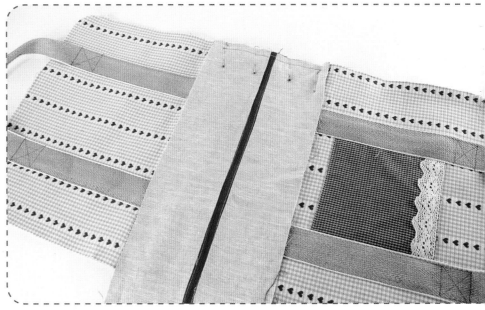

**14** Lay your bag face up, pin the zipped panel face down to the base, and sew across one end. Leave the other end for now.

**15** Pin the side of the zipped panel all the way around one side of the bag, and sew. If your fabric is too thick to pin, you can use quilters' clips.

**16** Pin and sew the other side of the zipped panel to the second side of the bag. Open the zip enough to turn and finally sew the base of the bag to the other end of the zipped panel. You will find that the zip needs trimming by about 2.5cm (1in). I allowed plenty to make sure the zip wasn't too short, as it is easier to shorten the zip than to try and add length to it! Stitch the remaining short side of the zipper panel to the bottom of the bag.

**17** Turn your bag the right way round.

**18** Push a bag foot through the base of the bag, close to each corner, and fix (see Bag feet, page 11). The feet secure all the layers of the bag base together. Cover them with another piece of fabric if you don't want to see them.

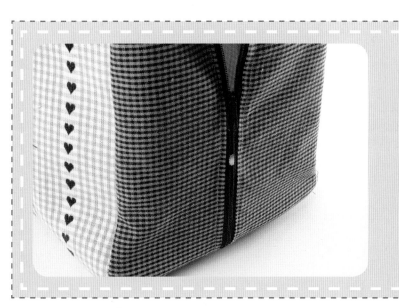

## Tip

If you don't want the zip to open all the way, place a spot of glue at the point where you want it to stop.

# Index